ROBIN RED BREAST

BY TRACEY CURTIS

<u>Other books in this series</u>

Lazy Bones

I'M In Love With The Cat

I'm Just An Ugly Flea

The Troublesome Bumblebee

Acknowledgment

For All Their Help In Making This Book I Thank

My husband
K.N..CURTIS

My Son
E.L.R..ABBOTT

ROBIN
RED
BREAST

I was out
the other
day in my
garden
Sewing
seed

Raking up
the soil
and pulling
up the
weeds

As I sat
down on
my bench
To have a
sip of tea

A little
robin red
breast
Flew down
in front of
me

He looked
so very
cheeky
As he sat
there by
my feet

He hopped
a little
closer
Then he
flew upon
the seat

I turned my
head so
slowly
And I didn't
make a
sound

His little
eyes were
blinking
As he
started
looking
round

He just
seemed so
contented
as he sat
there in the
sun

Then he
flew up on
a branch
To see
what I had
done

I slowly
held my
hand out
with some
birdseed in
my palm

I smiled
and said
now there
you go I
don't mean
you any
harm

Then all of
a sudden
he flew
down on
my hand

He really
was the
sweetest
thing and
his colours
were so
grand

Then he
turned and
looked at
me as if to
say hello

Thank you
kindly for
the food
but now I
have to go

With his
little head
a tilt
And his
little feet a
spray

He hopped
down on
the ground
again
And then
he flew
Away

I watched
him for a
moment till
he flew out
of sight

That little
robin red
breast
Was such
a sweet
delight

Printed in Great Britain
by Amazon

18244982R00031